Agassiz (L^s) Mr Valenciennes

souvenir de l'Auteur.

The primitive diversity and number of animals in Geological times

From the American Journal of Science and Arts, 2nd Series, Vol. XVII.—May, 1854.

THE
PRIMITIVE DIVERSITY
AND NUMBER OF ANIMALS IN
GEOLOGICAL TIMES.

By L. AGASSIZ.

There is a view generally entertained by naturalists and geologists that genera and species of animals and plants are greatly more numerous at the present age of the world than in any previous geological period. This seems to me an entire misconception of the character and diversity of the fossils which have been discovered in the different geological formations, and to rest upon estimates which are not made within the same limits, and with the same standard. Whenever a comparison of the diversity and number of fossils of any geological period has been made with those of the living animals and plants belonging to the same classes and families, it has been done under the tacit assumption which seems to me entirely unjustifiable, that the fossils formerly inhabiting our globe are known to the same extent as the animals which live at present upon its surface; while it should be well understood that however accurate our knowledge of fossils may be, it has been restricted, for each geological formation, to a few circumscribed areas. Comparisons of fossils with the living animals ought, therefore, to be limited to geographical districts corresponding in extent to those in which the fossils occur; or, more properly, a fossil fauna with all its local peculiarities ought to be compared with a *corresponding* fauna of the present period, and not with *all* the animals of the same class living at present *upon the whole surface* of the globe. And when this is done with sufficient care and proper allowance is made for the limited time during which investigations of fossils have been traced compared with that which has been almost everywhere devoted to the closer study of living animals, it will be seen that the number and diversity of species peculiar to each special fossil fauna is, in most instances, equal to those found to characterize zoological provinces of similar boundaries, at the present day. And this may be said of the fossil faunæ of all ages. In many instances the result is even quite the reverse of what is generally supposed to be the fact, for there are distinct fossil faunæ which have yielded much larger numbers of species, presenting a greater variety of types than any corresponding fauna in the present age. Some examples will justify this perhaps unexpected statement.

The number of species of shells which are found living along the shores of Europe, does not exceed six hundred. About six hundred species is again the number assigned to the whole basin of the Mediterranean, including both the European and African coasts. Now the most superficial comparison between them and the fossil species which occur in the lower tertiary beds in the vicinity of Paris, shows the latter to exceed twice that number; there are indeed twelve hundred species of fossil shells now known from the eocene beds in the immediate vicinity of Paris, affording, at once, a very striking evidence of the greater diversity and greater number of species of that geological period when compared even with those of a wider geographical area at the present day.

If it be objected that the variety of forms which occur in tropical faunæ is greater than that which we observe on the shores of our temperate regions, and that the temperature of the tertiary period having been warmer we may expect a larger number of fossil species from those deposits, I would only refer to local enumerations of marine shells from several tropical regions, to sustain my assertion that the number of fossil shells of the eocene beds of the *immediate vicinity of Paris*, is much greater than that of any local fauna of the present period, even within the tropics. A catalogue of not quite three hundred species of shells given by Dufo as occurring around the Sechelles Islands, the extent of which may fairly be compared with that of the lower tertiary beds around Paris, will suffice to show, that in a tropical local fauna the number of species known to exist in the present day is far inferior to the number of species known to have occurred during the deposition of the lower tertiary beds in the vicinity of Paris. Another catalogue by Sganzin, of the shells found about Mauritius, Bourbon and Madagascar, gives also less than 300 species for that extensive range of seas surrounding those islands. Let us further compare the results of the investigations of the shells of the Red Sea by Hemprich, Ehrenberg and Rüppel, and there again we find a smaller number, and a more limited variety of types than are found in the tertiary of Paris; for the whole basin of the Red Sea has thus far yielded only 400 species of shells. Let us finally take the most accurate survey of this kind we have of any shore, that of Panama by Prof. Adams, extending over 50° of latitude, 28° N. of the equator, and 22° S. of it, including the most favorable localities for the growth of shells in the Pacific under the tropics, and yet we shall find his list exceeding but little the number of 500 species. In this instance again we find that the advantage in number and variety is in favor of the tertiary period, and not of the present age. If a different result has been obtained by the estimates made before this, it is owing to the circumstance, that the *fossils known from a few localities within narrow geographical limits* were compared with the *living species known to occur upon the whole surface of the globe.* But let us trace these comparisons through other geological periods, with reference to other classes also, and we shall find in every instance, similar results. The tertiary fossils of Bordeaux, though less numerous in species than those of the eocene in the vicinity of Paris, will compare with any local fauna of the present period as favorably for variety and number of species as those of the lower tertiaries. This may be said, with the same certainty, of the tertiary shells of the Sub-appennine Hills, or of those of the English Crag of which we now possess a very complete list.

If from the tertiary periods we pass down to the cretaceous, do we not find in the deposits of Mæstricht, or in those of the age of the white chalk, a number and variety of shells as great as that which may be found on any shore or in any circumscribed marine basin of an extent at all comparable with that of the cretaceous beds within similar limits? Do we not find in the lower cretaceous strata such as the green sand or the Neocomien, other assemblages of the remains of Mollusks, which, in number and variety, are not inferior to those of the white chalk? The oolitic series, again, will stand a similar comparison quite as well. We need not even take the whole group of those deposits, but consider each subdivision of the Jurassic period by itself, and still we find in every one, local faunæ of Mollusks, assuming of course, a different character from those of the cretaceous or tertiary, but nevertheless sufficiently diversified to admit of an estimate, as advantageous, with respect to the points under consideration, and to the local faunæ of the present day as to the cretaceous assemblages of fossils, or those of the tertiary period. Of course, in accordance with the peculiar character of the age, different families prevail in these different periods; the Cephalopoda are extremely numerous and surprisingly diversified during the cretaceous and oolitic periods; while they dwindle down to a few representatives in the tertiaries, and so with other families. The shells found in the deposits of the new red sandstone period, of the coal period, and of the still earlier ages, are perhaps less numerous on the whole, though they can hardly be said to be less diversified; for, the extinct forms which occur among them, are quite an equivalent to the variety of their families which have lived during more recent periods; and the daily increase of the species found in the different palæozoic deposits shows that, even in point of numbers those ancient faunæ may, even in the present state of our knowledge, be compared with local faunæ of similar extent at the present day.

Desirous of making the most accurate comparison possible between the *subdivisions* of the paleozoic formations of the state of New York with *local faunæ of similar extent* in the present seas, I have requested Professor J. Hall to furnish me with summary indications respecting the results of his extensive investigations in this field, and I have obtained from him the following statement:

"I regard the *Potsdam and Calciferous Sandstone* as disconnected with the groups above, forming of themselves with their fauna (not yet well known in this country) a distinct geological period. The entire number of species thus far known in these rocks, admitting all of Owen's species, is however only twenty-six."

"The *Chazy limestone* has 45 species restricted to itself, and one other species which is also known in the Black River Limestone. The *Birdseye limestone* has 19 species restricted to itself and two others which pass upwards. The *Black River limestone* has 13 species restricted to itself, and one common to it, and the Chazy limestone, one common to it and Birdseye, and one common to it and the Trenton, and one other which is common to the beds below and above, extending into the Hudson River group," making together 81 species for these three sets of beds.

"The *Trenton limestone* has 188 species restricted to itself, and 30 species passing upwards into the Hudson River group. The entire number of species known as occurring in the Trenton limestone, including those which occur in rocks above and below is about 230. This statement includes some species discovered since the publication of the 1st volume of the Palæontology of New York, and which would make the restricted species about 200."

"The *Hudson River group*, including Utica slate, has about 60 restricted species, besides those which are common to it and the rocks below, making altogether about 100 species."

"You will observe that the development of life at the Trenton period, has been far the most marked, though it is true that this formation is much thicker than either of the preceding limestones, the Chazy being the thickest, and the Black River the thinnest of the three below the Trenton."

"In that portion of the upper Silurian period included in the 2d vol. of the Palæontology of New York, the fossils of the Medina Sandstone, Clinton group, Niagara and Onondaga Salt groups, amount to 341. *Medina and Clinton groups* 123 species. *Niagara and Onondaga Salt group*, 218 species."

"The Medina Sandstone and arenaceous beds of the Clinton group contain 50 species, leaving for the calcareous beds of the Clinton group 73 species, which, added to the 218 species of the Niagara and Onondaga Salt groups, give 291 species as the total number of species of the calcareous beds of these groups. The Niagara is here the more important period, and though not thicker than either of the others, contains about 200 species restricted to itself. Of the Niagara group 67 species are Corals and Bryozoa. Of the 73 species from the calcareous beds of the Clinton group, 19 are Corals and Bryozoa."

"In the *lower Helderberg group*, including the Water lime, Pentamerus limestone, Delthyris Shaly limetone, and upper Pentamerus limestone, I expect to describe about 200 species, exclusive of Corals and Bryozoa, of which I know already about fifty species."

"The *Oriskany Sandstone* may contain about 60 species of fossils altogether, perhaps less."

"In the *upper Helderberg group*, which is the next great Calcareous formation, I anticipate a less number of species except Corals and Bryozoa, of which there are more than 100 species in New York and the western localities. Of all that is yet known in these limestones besides Corals and Bryozoa, it would be unsafe for me to estimate more than 100 species."

"From the *Hamilton*, *Portage* and *Chemung groups* I anticipate at least 300 species within New York, and I shall not be surprised if more complete investigations produce double that number in New York and the West."

"The number of species given here I regard as only approximate. I hope this general statement may meet your present requirement, but I regret that I cannot now give you more definite information, particularly regarding the Upper Helderberg. I give you from this and the higher groups an estimate based on the species known to me at the present time; but my final investigations always reveal a greater number than I anticipate."

These statements of Professor Hall place already each of the principal group of rocks of the state of New York in the category of distinct independent successive faunæ, equivalent each to as many local faunæ of the present period, for we may repeat that the fauna of the Sechelles contains only 258 species, and that of

Mauritius, Bourbon and Madagascar, 275. Nay, upon 3000 miles of coast along the western shores of the American continent, within the tropics only twice the number of living species have been obtained as occur respectively in each successive greater subdivision of the paleozoic system within the narrow limits of the state of New York only. (See above the results of Professor Adams's investigations upon the coast of Panama.)

It is a most unexpected and very significant coincidence that the late admirable investigations of Elie de Beaumont upon the mountain systems, have led him to the recognition of nearly ten times as many periods of great disturbance in the physical constitution of the earth's surface, as he himself knew twenty-five years ago, each attended by the upheaval of as many mountain chains, differing in their main direction. The investigations of palæontologists having an entirely different character, and founded upon facts which until recently have apparently had only a remote connection with the other series of phenomena, have nevertheless brought them at about the same time to like conclusions respecting animal life, showing that the periods of disappearance and renovation of organized beings upon earth, have been much more frequent than could be supposed even ten years ago, each set having probably been characteristic of one of those long periods of comparative rest, intervening between two great successive geological cataclysms.

What is true of Mollusca, may be said of all other classes. Among Radiata, are not the coral reefs of the palæozoic ages as rich in species as any coral reef of the Pacific? Let us even compare the most extensive list of corals yet given as belonging to any circumscribed locality,—those of the Red Sea as described by Ehrenberg,—those of the Feejee Islands as described by Prof. J. D. Dana,—and let us inquire whether the palæozoic rocks of the state of New York do not show as great a variety and as large a number of species in their successive reefs. Again, the coral reefs of the oolitic period in Normandy, or in the Jura of Switzerland, and the Alp of Wurtemberg, have they not increased our lists of fossils as largely and introduced into our zoological works as various forms as are known from any of the most diversified coral regions in the world at the present day?

Passing from the corals to the Echinoderms, the question may be reversed, and it may be fairly asked whether there is any sea shore extending over tens and tens of degrees of longitude and latitude even under the tropics which has yielded as large a number of those Radiata, as occur in almost any of the geological formations? The number of Crinoids found in the single set of beds known under the name of Niagara limestone, equals the whole number of Echinoderms found around all the coast of the United States. The Crinoids, Echini, and Star-fishes of the oolitic period, or any of the subdivisions of that formation, surpass the number of species of that class which may be gathered around the coast of entire continents in the present day. The diversity of forms of these animals comparing them with those of the cretaceous periods, is equally great, though the Crinoids begin to diminish in number. But the variety of Spatangoids and Clypeastroids which come into play, compensate largely for the diminution of the family of Crinoids.

The type of Articulata may seem, in the present condition of our knowledge, to form an unanswerable objection to the broad statement I have made above, for the hundred thousands of insects which are known in the present creation will hardly allow a comparison with the fossils. But let us examine upon the principles by which we have been guided in the preceding computations, what is the true state of things respecting the occurrence of Articulata in former geological periods. We can, of course, hardly expect to find worms well preserved in geological formations, on account of the softness of their body, which will scarcely allow of preservation to a greater degree than Medusæ. But a few instances in which impressions of these animals have been found justifies the assertion that they existed as well in former periods as now. The impressions of Medusæ found in the lithographic limestone of Solenhofen, which are preserved in the Museum of Carlsruhe, not only carry back the existence of this class to the Jurassic period, but justify the question whether a large number of the fossil polypi from older periods, which have been described as belonging to that class, are not in reality nurses of Medusæ similar to the Campanulariæ, and Sertulariæ of the present day, which are now known to be no Polyps, but one of the alternate generations of Medusæ. And as for the worms, we find in each geological formation, from the oldest to the most recent, fossil Serpulæ, or similar solid cases of worms in as large numbers as we find these animals any where at the present day. And where the existence of Serpulæ is established by such unquestionable evidence as that of their calcareous cases, are we not justified in the inference that those entirely naked worms which are found every where existing with Serpulæ, had also their corresponding representatives during former geological periods?

With the class of Crustacea the difficulty in the comparison is already less; for, in the tertiary beds of Sheppy there have been found a variety of lobsters, shrimps and crabs, which would favorably compare with the crab fauna of any limited shore in the present day; and I doubt very much whether such a variety of Crustacea could be collected any where on a shore of equal extent to that of the white chalk of Sussex, as Dr. Mandell has uncovered in the vicinity of Lewes. For a comparison of the Crustacea of the oolitic period, I would only refer the skeptic to the monograph of the Crustacea of Solenhofen by Count Münster, who has figured from that single locality more species than are known in the whole basin of the Mediterranean, excluding the minute species which have not yet been sought for among the fossils.

In earlier geological ages, during the deposition of the coal and other palæozoic rocks, the class of Crustacea presents a very different character. The gigantic Entomostraca and the extinct family of Trilobites take the place of the lobsters and crabs of later periods. But palæontological works illustrating the fossils of Sweden, Russia, Bohemia, England and France, have made us acquainted with as great a variety of species of those families as are found of the later representatives of the class in more modern deposits. So that among Articulata the class of Crustacea can be said to have been, at all periods, as largely represented, and to have shown as great a variety of forms as occur any where within similar limits in the present time.

The carcinological fauna of the whole Indian Ocean scarcely exceeds in variety or number of species that of Bohemia alone, as it is now known by the admirable investigations of Mr. de Barande.

From their minuteness and general structure, Insects might be excepted in such a comparison without affording a sufficient argument against the view I have taken of the subject, even if insects had nowhere been found in large numbers in a fossil state. For it must be plain that their preservation requires more favorable circumstances than the preservation of other animals more largely provided with solid parts. But though the fossil insects have not been sufficiently investigated in all geological formations, have we not several examples which show that in some geological periods, at least, they were as numerous as in the present day? The beautiful Monograph of Behrens, of the insects which occur in Amber, shows how varied these animals were during the period of the formation of that gum, and the unparalleled investigations of Professor Oswald Heer upon the insects of Oeningen and Radeboy have furnished us with means of comparisons which show that during the deposition of the Molasse of Switzerland, the insects were as numerous and as diversified there as they are any where in our day, within similar boundaries. And the fragmentary information which we already possess upon the insects of Aix in Provence, and those of Oeningen will justify the expectation that insects will finally be found very numerous in all the geological periods from that of the carboniferous deposit to the present day; that is to say, ever since terrestrial vegetation has had an extensive development. The discoveries by Hugh Miller of true trees in the old red sandstone will justify the prophecy that insects will be found, some day or other, even among palæozoic rocks older than the coal period.

But what of the Vertebrata? Is there not evidence, that, at the present day, they are more diversified and more numerous? Here again I answer, decidedly, No; granting only that there are periods during which the higher classes of these types did not exist, and that therefore, as a type, the vertebrata of the present day are more diversified; but the individual classes, from the time of their appearance have been in each former period, as numerous and even as various as they are at present.

Let us apply to these the same measure which we have applied to the Radiata, Mollusca, and Articulata, to justify this assertion, which seems so completely at variance with our knowledge of fossil vertebrata. Fishes occur, as is well known, in all geological formations. But should we compare the fossil fishes of each geological period as they are known from a few localities, with the whole number of fishes which exist all over the world in our day? It would be as unphilosophical as it would be inconsistent with our knowledge of the geographical distribution of animals. Like all other living beings, fishes are located within definite boundaries, and it will be but fair to compare the fossil species of a given locality with the special Ichthyological faunæ which occur in different oceans, or in different fresh-water basins. Now with this rule we may institute a comparison of the fossil fishes with the living ones, with reference to their number as well as to their variety.

The number of species of fossil fishes known at present from the tertiary deposits, in a single spot, upon the Island of Sheppy, is greater than the number of fishes which have been gathered around the coast of any of the islands of the Pacific Ocean, as far as we know the local Ichthyological faunæ of those regions; it is as great, nearly, as the whole number of fishes known from the shores of Great Britain. The same may be said of the fishes of Mount Bolca, or of Mount Lebanon, or of those of the white chalk of England, or of those of Solenhofen, or of those of the lias of Lyme Regis; and if we pass to older deposits, to the old red sandstone even,—thanks to Mr. Miller, and to the investigations of other British and Russian geologists,—do we not know from that old formation as many fishes as from any of the more recent ones, or from any circumscribed marine basin? and is not the variety which occurs among them at each period as great, though of a different character in each, as the variety which occurs at the present day? So that it can be fairly said, that at all periods, fishes have presented as great a variety of forms, and as numerous species, as under corresponding circumstances at the present day.

The class of Reptiles will allow similar conclusions, for though the giants of the class have chiefly been studied, do they not indicate an abundance, and a variety of these animals during the

2

upper secondary formations, as great as in any tropical region? and have we not sufficient indications among the tertiaries to be justified in expecting that they also will turn out to be more numerous than they are now known to be?

The class of Birds seems to form an exception in this view. But there seems to be particular reason why the bones of birds should be more liable to destruction and decomposition than those of other vertebrata. And whoever has traced the discoveries made recently among the fossils of this class, will certainly not insist upon a supposed scarcity of birds in former periods, but rather be inclined to admit that the limited number now known is to be ascribed to the deficiency of our knowledge rather than to a want of these animals in earlier formations, indications of their presence having been ascertained for several tertiary formations, for cretaceous deposits, and even for deposits belonging to periods older than the chalk.

Fossil Mammalia are comparatively too well known to call for many remarks, after what has been said above. Let us only remember that the number of fossil species found in Brazil alone equals the whole number of Mammalia known to live at present in that country; that the fossil Mammalia of New Holland compare already favorably with the living species of that continent; and that the locality of Montmartre alone has yielded as many large Mammalia as occur all over Europe, and the Mauvaises Terres in Nebraska as many as may be found in North America now. So that, if we grant simply that among vertebrata the diversity has been increasing with the successive introduction of their different classes, the number and diversity of these different classes at each period has been as great as it is at present.

These facts are of the utmost importance with reference to the great question of the order of succession and gradation of animals in the different geological periods. They cut away forever one of the arguments upon which the asserters of the development theory have insisted most emphatically. Before it could be granted that the great variety of types which occur at any later periods has arisen from a successive differentiation of a few still earlier types, it should be shown that in reality in former periods the types are fewer and less diversified; and we have now shown that this is so far from being the case, that in many instances the reverse is really true. I have already attempted elsewhere to show in outlines what is the real order of succession of the great types of the animal kingdom, I need not therefore repeat here what may be gathered from the diagram at the head of the Zoological Text Book I have published jointly with Dr. Gould. I shall limit myself to a few more general remarks upon the special difficulties involved in a more thorough investigation of the subject.

The study of the order of succession and gradation of the organized beings which have inhabited our globe at different periods, presents indeed difficulties of more than one kind. Unhappily these difficulties have seldom been all considered in their natural connection by those who have ventured to consider the subject in its whole extent; thus presenting certain results as general which would require various qualifications to be true. In comparing fossils of one and the same or of different geological formations, it is in reality not enough to ascertain their true geological horizon, which we may call the *chronological element* of the enquiry; it is equally important that the differences or resemblances arising from the geographical distribution over the wide expanse of the whole surface of the globe, which we may call the *topographic element* of the question, should be also considered, for it is already known that within certain limits the same differences and resemblances which are observed at present between the animals inhabiting different parts of the globe existed already in former geological periods. We must therefore become acquainted with the *general biological character* of the epoch as well as with the *local faunæ* of each period. The tertiary faunæ of New Holland and the Brazils for instance, resemble more closely the living faunæ of those parts of the world than they resemble one another. Our lists of fossils teem with chronological errors of the worst kind, arising partly from false identifications of strata, which in reality belong to different periods, but the fossils of which are thus represented as having inhabited our globe simultaneously, when in reality they may have been separated by long periods of time, and existed upon earth under very different physical conditions. This chronological confusion is further increased by the too extensive limits frequently assigned by geologists to the successive groups of rocks forming the crust of our globe. For instance, when the cretaceous or the oolitic formations are considered respectively as indivisible natural groups, and the fossils of all their subdivisions are enumerated in one single list as the inhabitants of a long period, an infinitude of anachronisms are presented to the mind, which no special mention of localities can rectify; and until the fossils of each of the natural subdivisions of these formations shall have been grouped together and compared carefully, as I have attempted to do it in my Monographs of the *Trigoniæ* and of the *Myæ* of Switzerland and the adjoining countries, or as Al. d'Orbigny has done it upon a much larger scale in his Paléontologie Françoise, no correct ideas can be formed respecting the succession of animals and plants characteristic of these long successive periods. I do not believe there is a single palæontologist, whose opinion is worth having, who can suppose, at this day, that any of the animals, the remains of which are buried in the lias, lived simultaneously with those of the inferior oolite, or these with those of the Oxford clay, or these with those of the upper division of the so-called oolitic formation. The same may be said of the different natural subdivisions of the cretaceous formation, and of the subdivisions introduced of late among the palæozoic rocks, by Sir Roderick Murchison, and Professor Sedgwick, and in America, by Professor J. Hall.

But even after this separation of the fossils, the synchronism of which may be fully established, our task is only fairly laid open, for then must begin the zoological identification of all the species, which has to be correct in every respect before general conclusions can be drawn from it.

In the first place the *specific identity* of organic remains is not so easily ascertained as many geologists would seem to suppose, if we judge from their statements; but unless the validity of a species is sanctioned by a practiced Zoölogist, it can not be taken as a basis for sound generalizations in reference to questions of a purely zoological character. The number of false identifications which have been accumulated in geological works is truly frightful. It would be however very unjust to accuse geologists in general of inaccuracy for this, the fault is mostly to be traced to other parties from which the names were obtained. It should only be understood that the materials thus accumulated are no longer fit to be used for the discussion of the questions which have been raised with the modern progress of geology, and that a thorough revision of *all* the identifications made in former years is imperatively demanded by the modern progress of palæontology. It would be however sometimes amusing, were it not actually distressing, to see the manner in which some geologists deal with fossils, considering them simply as the characteristics of certain rocks, and hardly yet dreaming that there may be such a thing as a special zoology of the different geological periods, and that during each, local faunæ may have existed with peculiar animals, &c. The ideas about characteristic fossils are still very crude, and nothing is more absurd than the complaints about unnecessary multiplication of genera and species; as if both genera and species had not a natural existence, independent of the estimates of naturalists. It would be just as reasonable for astronomers to complain of the great number of stars, as for geologists to object to the investigations of zoologists, on the ground that they lead to the "making" of "*too many species.*"

The difficulty with reference to the identification of species is three-fold: 1, different species may be considered as identical, 2, specimens of the same species in different states of preservation, or of different age, or sex, &c., may be considered as distinct species, or 3, the same species may have been described by different authors under different names, and their identity afterwards overlooked by later writers. Who does not see what amount of error may accrue from the indiscriminate use of materials which are not first submitted to a very critical revision in these different respects, not to speak of the general difficulty of agreeing upon the limits of specific differences. With regard to this last point, however, I would say that whosoever would only use in discussing general questions materials revised candidly with the same principles, could not fail to obtain at least uniform results. And when the results of investigations made upon materials corrected in different ways by different authors are compared with one another, if these differences are kept in view, the disagreement in the results would not be found so great as it might otherwise seem. The astronomers and physicists have long learned to correct their observations before using them, and to take into consideration what they call the personal equation of different observers; are we never to learn from them a lesson in the estimation of our respective investigations, and shall our facts for ever be used without being first corrected for all the possible causes of error and disagreement? As long as there are differences of opinion respecting the natural limits of genera and species, is it not absolutely necessary to reduce or expand the scale applied to the investigations of different authors, when using them for the same purposes, exactly in the same manner as thermometric observations made with the scales of Reaumur or Celsius or Fahrenheit are reduced to the same standard, before being compared.

In the second place, *species must be referred to genera circumscribed within the same limits*, before they can fairly be compared or at least lead to trustworthy general results. As long as certain bivalve shells of the carboniferous and oolitic series were referred to the genus *Unio*, it could appear that the family of *Naiades* began its existence at a very early period; but since the oolitic species of this kind have been ascertained to differ essentially from our freshwater shells, and to constitute by themseles a natural genus more closely allied to Crassatella than to Unio, nobody thinks any longer of looking for Unios in *marine deposits*. As long as certain fossil fishes of the Zechstein and Lias were referred to the genera Esox and Cyprinus, the families of which these genera are the types could be supposed to have extended their range far beyond the tertiary formations, before which however no one of their representatives is to be found. Before the Spatangoids were divided into natural genera, the genus Spatangus was mentioned among the fossils of the oolitic as well as the cretaceous and tertiary formations; now it is restricted to the last among the fossils and found also among the living. I do not believe that a single genuine species of Gorgonia is found among the fossil Polypi, and yet that genus appears in the lists of fossils from the palæozoic period to the present time.

Since it is not my intention to enter here upon a special criticism of the innumerable errors of this kind, still to be found in even modern lists of fossils, I shall not multiply my examples. These may be sufficient to show how important a correct *generic* identification of the fossils may be in the estimation of the order of succession of organized beings; and I cannot but lament the utter want of consideration evinced even by many distinguished palæontologists in this respect, who seem to think that the knowledge of species is sufficient in itself to a proper appreciation of the order of creation, and that genera are arbitrary divisions established by naturalists merely for the sake of facilitating the study of species, as if the more general relations of living beings to one another were not as definitely regulated in all their degrees by the same thinking mind, as the ultimate relations of individuals to one another.

In the third place *the natural affinities of genera should be ascertained.* Unless the genera are referred to the families to which they truly belong, unless the rank of these families in their respective classes is positively determined, unless the peculiarities of structure which characterizes them is taken as the foundation of such an arrangement and further corroborated by the mode of development of their respective types, it would be a hopeless task to attempt to determine the order of succession of the fossils in different geological formations. Before the Crinoids which Lamark placed along the Polyps had been referred to the class of Echinoderms, nobody could have understood the beautiful gradation so fully ascertained now, which may be traced through all geological formations among these animals. Before it was ascertained that the little animal described by Thompson under the name of Pentacrinus europeus, as a living Crinoid, for which DeBlainville established the genus Phytocrinus, is in reality the young of a Comatula, nobody could have suspected the wonderful relations which exist between the changes animals now living undergo during their growth, and the order of succession of entire classes of animals during successive geological ages. As long as the natural position of Trilobites remained doubtful in the animal kingdom, the characters of the prototypes of the class of Crustacea could not be appreciated. Who does not see how impossible it was for those who classified the Trilobites with the Chitons to arrive at any sound results respecting the gradation and order of succession of these animals? Whilst now they are beautifully linked to the Macrura of the Trias, by the gigantic Entomostraca of the Devonian and Carboniferous periods. Again, the knowledge of the embryology of Crustacea gives us a key to a correct appreciation of the early appearance of the Macrura and the late introduction of the Brachyura. The removal of the Bryozoa from among Polypi to the class of Mollusks, will entirely change the aspect and relations of the faunæ of the paleozoic rocks. How different, again, would the order of succession of Mollusks appear, were we to adhere to Cuvier's view of separating the Brachiopods, as a class, from the other Acephala, to which they are now more correctly referred The vexed question of the period of appearance of Dicotyledonous plants in the geological series would have been settled long ago, had it been placed upon its real foundation. It is not in reality to be argued upon palæontological evidence chiefly, for it resolves itself in the main into a botanical question, and the definite answer must depend upon the position finally assigned by botanists to the families of Coniferæ and Cycadeæ. If these natural orders of plants are really allied to the Dicotyledonæ, then this type begins with the palæozoic rocks in the Devonian system, and there is no gradation in the order of succession of plants during geological times. But if the view of Brongniart is more correct, if the Coniferæ and Cycadeæ have to be separated from the Dicotyledonæ as Gymnospermæ, and if moreover these latter should prove, as I believe they are, inferior even to the Monocotyledoneæ, then we may at once recognize in the vegetable kingdom a similar gradation of types as among animals. These examples may suffice to show what is required for a proper investigation of the order of succession of organized beings in the course of time, and how little confidence the investigations in this field deserve, which have not been made with due reference to all the points mentioned above. It is indeed only in the classes, the structure and embryology of which is equally well understood, we are able to discover the laws regulating the succession of animals and plants in geological formations, and our knowledge is at present still too imperfect to carry the investigation into all families of the animal kingdom. And yet enough is known to leave no doubt as to the final result; we may confidently await the time when the glory of the wonderful order of creation shall be fully revealed to us, and this may stimulate us to renewed efforts, since the success depends entirely upon our own exertions.

The geographical distribution of animals began only to be studied long after systematic zoology had made considerable progress, but even to this day the limits of the faunæ are nowhere circumscribed with any kind of precision, the principles upon which they might be determined are in many respects questionable, and a large number of animals are daily described without any reference to their natural distribution upon the earth; though much has already been done since Buffon to place this branch of our knowledge upon a better foundation, and especially to ascertain the laws regulating the geographical distribution of certain classes and families considered isolately. The point which requires now particular attention, is the combination of these different types within definite regions, and their common circumscription within natural zoological provinces. This study would be particularly important with reference to the comparison of the local faunæ of former geological periods with those of the present creation. But since the latter even are comparatively little known, we must be satisfied to wait for the time when thorough comparisons shall be possible between the local faunæ of each and all geological periods *inter se*, and with those of other periods.

In closing this digression, I may sum up my criticism upon palæontological investigations, by saying that any generalization respecting the succession of organized beings which is not based upon materials in which the synchronism and succession of species and their geographical distribution is not duly considered, and in which the identification of species is not made with reference to sound zoological principles, with due regard to the equal limitation of genera, and also with reference to our improved classifications in zoology, is not fit to be trusted. All species taken into consideration should undergo a revision with reference to their chronology, their topography and their zoology, and in the last point of view the range and natural limitation as well as identity of the species, their generic affinities and their zoological classification should be equally tested.

Returning now to the main subject of this paper, I have further to say that the very fact that certain stratified rocks, even among the oldest formations, are almost entirely made up of fragments of organized beings, should long ago have satisfied the most skeptical that both *animal and vegetable life was as active and profusely scattered upon the whole globe, at all times and during all geological periods, as it is now.* No coral reef in the Pacific contains a larger amount of organic debris than some of the limestone deposits of the tertiary, of the cretaceous, or of the oolitic, nay even of the palæozoic periods, and the whole vegetable carpet covering the present surface of the globe, even if we were to consider only the most luxurious vegetation of the tropics, and leave entirely out of consideration the whole expanse of the ocean, as well as those tracks of land where under less favorable circumstances the growth of plants is more reduced, would not form one single seam of workable coal to be compared to the many thick beds contained in the rocks of the Carboniferous period alone.

www.ingramcontent.com/pod-product-compliance
Lightning Source LLC
LaVergne TN
LVHW021426110826
845150LV00007B/2102

* 9 7 8 1 4 2 5 5 0 8 3 2 6 *